It Will All Come Out in the Wash

A country boy's look at everyday life

Bob Baker

This book is for everyone out there that wakes up in the morning and needs a little nudge to put everything into perspective, and to remind them of what is really important in life.

All original writings by
Bob Baker

Photography courtesy of
Jill Baker

It Will All Come Out in The Wash

INTRODUCTION

I'm just an old country boy raised in a small southern town. My father was accidently killed by a gun shot when I was a young boy. My mother became the true hero in my life by assuming the role of both father and mother of six young children with little money. She never asked for a handout and taught us all that life isn't easy. If you want something, you better be willing to sacrifice and work for it.

I look at life in black and white with the opinion that everything we get out of life is a direct result of what we are willing to contribute, WITH A LITTLE BIT OF HUMOR THROWN IN. We all make our own decisions, and some are going to be good and some bad. We are all faced with challenges whether financial, medical, or personal but how you choose to handle those are up to you!

Like my mother once told me when I had a problem "Don't worry about it as IT WILL ALL COME OUT IN THE WASH".

From My World to Yours,
Bob Baker

Table of Contents

Page

10 **A Home**
12 **Coffee in My Hand**
14 **Bright Blue Morning Sky**
16 **Don't Even Take a Map**
18 **Give Up Which is Sad**
20 **Grandma's House**
22 **America Today**
24 **Helping Hand**
26 **Last Thing You See**
28 **Marble Bench**
30 **Mountain Fire and Memories**
32 **If Life Had a Re-Write**
33 **Son for Evermore**
35 **Waves on the Pier**
37 **Times with Friends and Family**
39 **Hurricane in Florida**
40 **Parents not Guns**
42 **When Those Towers Fell**
44 **An Electric Car**
45 **Weeds in The Garden**
47 **Respect is it Still Here**
48 **Pauper or a King**
50 **What If**
52 **This Old House was Spared**
54 **The Love Drifts Away**
55 **The Florida Pines**
56 **Surely Fade Away**
58 **Mother's Day Upon Us**
61 **What A Grandfather Should Be**
63 **Best Meal I Ever Ate**
65 Live for Today

Page

67	If We Knew It Was Our Last
70	Calluses and Dirty Hands
72	Growing Up in a Small Town
73	How Time Flies
74	Groves Have Gone Away
76	Front Porch
77	Moments
79	Weathered and Frail
80	What Shall I Do
81	Exercise He Said
83	I Don't Know the Pronouns
84	Song in Our Mind
85	Eyes from the Heart
86	Rain Like the Memories
87	Money on the Way
88	Hard to Endure
89	Ice Cream truck
90	Old Box of Memories
92	Roadside Cross
93	Vincent's Five and Dime
94	Down on Your Knees
95	Get Them Out of the Way
96	Labor Day
98	Opry House and Soda Shop
101	Whistle Stop Café
102	Under the Bridge
103	My Life Path
104	Ride in My Mind
106	Coming Home
108	Country Buffet
109	Family

Page

110   Coconut Soap
112   No Longer A Swing
113   Family Slip By
114   Pride In What You Have
115   Button Fly Jeans
116   Travel Light
118   Smiles
120   Rocks In The River
121   Forever Cry
122   Moon Pie
123   Time
124   Closing

PREFACE

Thank you to everyone that enjoy and take the time to send me your comments on my writings. Nothing makes my day better than when I receive a note saying how one of my writings hit home and let someone know they were not alone in their struggle. I get my inspiration from everyday occurrences, whether it's something I hear in conversation, see on TV, read or maybe something I see on the side of a back country road or city subway.

Life isn't always easy for any of us. At some point, we will all experience problems in our life whether they be family, illness or financial. Hell, most, if like me will experience them all. But remember we all learn most of life's worthwhile lessons from the hardships not the good things that happen.

So, sit back and enjoy my thoughts that I've put into words and maybe the one you read just might be what fits your problems today.

Remember, live life one day at a time and like my Momma always said "IT WILL ALL COME OUT IN THE WASH"

From My World to Yours,
Bob Baker

This is for you, Momma

A Home

We all have different opinions of what makes a house a
home
They all may look a little different in every town we may
roam

As we drive from town to town, throughout this vast great
land
We will see different kinds of houses, from New York to
Dixieland

Now some houses may be beautiful with a painted white
picket fence
While others may be in need of repair that to us might
make no sense

But we will never know what lies behind that front door
and those walls
The love, fear or maybe the misfortune of the residents in
them all

Some people feel that what makes a home is how big the
structure stands
Where in fact what makes a house a home is the family's
loving hands

It doesn't matter if the house has four rooms or maybe
even ten
The house will only become a home from whatever lies
within

continued

A home is a place where love and joy and memories take
first place
A place where children want to come home too for it is
their safe space

A home is a loving place no matter if it is big or small
Whether it sits on a quiet little street or high rise standing
tall

So, if you want your house to truly become a loving home
today
It can only come from your heart within and not from
where you stay

Coffee in my Hand

I love this time of year when the weather begins to change
How fast it goes from Summer to Fall always seems so
strange

You go from sleeping in a closed-up house running the
cold AC
To sleeping with the windows open feeling the night's
cool autumn breeze

In Florida, it goes from walking outside and suddenly
covered in sweat
To rocking on the screen porch and being as comfortable
as it gets

The squirrels are busy in the yard digging for acorns to
store for winter food
I'm just sitting with my coffee in hand as the sun rises in
complete solitude

I sure do love when the weather cools down, it creates
happiness in the air
People are in a much better mood and you see them out
everywhere

People here put on their sweaters, and take walks around
our little town
It's like people move at a slower pace and loose that hot
weather frown

continued

We take the time to walk around the lake and stop and say
hello
People seem to enjoy this weather as the Fall breeze
lightly blows

The seasons in this southern state don't change as in the
states up north
But when it gets to 60 degrees you can bet we'll be
bundled up of course

So, as the seasons turn from Summer to Fall in states
throughout this great land
I'll sit here on the porch rocking under my blanket with
my coffee in my hand

Bright Blue Morning Sky

As I set out this morning driving and gazed at the road
ahead
What I was admiring made me forget where the highway
led

It was something that was marvelous, and I was fortunate
to see
An unusual blue sky that was cloudless and beautiful
beyond belief

I found myself captivated and enchanted at such a
beautiful site
And couldn't help but be thankful for a sky so blue and
bright

As I gazed, I started thinking about all of life's true
fulfilling gifts
Some we take for granted like viewing a waterfall flowing
over a cliff

As we go through life, we see things of beauty as we head
out every day
But sadly, in our busy world we just pass them by as we
hurry on our way

When you look back at all the things you passed by and
were in a hurry and missed
Things like when you saw the mother and baby deer
standing there in the morning mist

continued

There are beautiful things in nature or maybe the family in
your home
We will always cherish if we live our life in color instead
of monochrome   15

So just try to slow down a little and view the world as it
goes by
And you too, might get to see a BRIGHT BLUE
MORNING SKY

Don't Even Take a Map

Some people feel in life they need a bunch of expensive
toys
Like fancy boats and exotic cars to fulfill their need for joy

Some people get their fun from expensive lavish trips
Maybe taken on the Orient Express or on a fancy ship

Now we all like to have some fun and enjoy the finer
things in life
We need the time to just recharge, and relieve a little of the
strife

We all can't always just pack up and head out at any time
Or jump in a fancy boat or car and leave at the drop of a
dime

But we can all take just a little time on any Sunday
afternoon
To get in the car and take a drive and explore like Daniel
Boone

You don't have to trek through the forest or climb a
mountain wall
You can find things on an old back road that bring
pleasure to us all

It may be the little deserted cemetery lying beneath the old
oak trees
Or the road with branches hanging across the road full of
autumn's colored leaves

continued

You may find a road that travels past a meadow full of
wildflowers
If you are lucky, you'll see it during one of summer's light
rain showers

There is nothing more fun than to drive down a little
lonesome country road
Not knowing or even caring where the little road ends or
even where it goes

You may see a little run-down shack that was someone's
home many years ago
But now it no longer houses them but has become a
beautiful place for vines to grow

So next Sunday afternoon pack a picnic and put on your
favorite cap
Roll down your windows and drive the back roads and
don't even take a map

Give up Which is Sad

Today I was sitting at a traffic light on a small-town, two-
lane road
When standing on the corner was a little woman with a
heavy load

She looked to be aging from the weather and the harsh
Summer sun
But not from playing on the beach as most people do for
fun

Her shoes were worn and tattered and T-shirt covered with
dirt
I could tell by the way she was standing her feet they
seemed to hurt

This tired little woman no telling how many miles she has
roamed
How wonderful it might be for her to have a bath and her
hair combed

Then maybe that isn't what she seeks but just a life on the
street alone
The reason she is pushing the cart with her stuff to me
remains unknown

As the light turned green and I moved along with my daily
life
I couldn't stop thinking she someone's mother, daughter,
or their wife

continued

Maybe her family was searching for her and wondering
where she has gone
But then again maybe no one cares and are just glad she
has moved along

Life's not easy and gives us many turns, some are good
and some are bad
Sometimes people just can't take the fight and just give up,
which is sad

Grandma's House

A little house sits in shambles there on the lonely street
It used to be a happy place where family all would meet

The little rooms of this house were always filled with joy
Where, as kids we would play outside not needing any toy

There was no greater time in life than when cousins did
arrive
It was like Christmas time and this little house really came
alive

Grandma would be in the kitchen fixing a true southern
feast
And we as kids were running and rolling around under
Grandpa's feet

We would get down to our underwear and get the garden
hose
Squirting both boys and girls getting soaked from head to
toes

When the nighttime fell upon us, we would all pile into
one bed
And make plans for with excitement for the days that lie
ahead

To most people that see this old house it's just a falling
down old shack
But to me it's all the memories of fun at Grandma's house
that just keep coming back

America Today

Have you ever really taken time to reflect on everything in
your life
The number of good and happy things, compared to the
amount of sadness, pain and strife

We all will leave our homes today and venture out into the
world
Some of us will move at a slow crawling pace and others
in a frantic whirl

The one thing we in America will all have, and thankfully
be able to share
Is the ability to chase our own dreams without fear,
persecution or despair

Some of us out there are Doctors and others love to farm
the land
Some want to be on stage while others give needy a
helping hand

No matter what the news reports or politicians they portray
There will never be a greater place to live than in America
today

America gives us all the opportunity to follow our path
and dreams
Sometimes it may not be easy and at times impossible it
seems

continued

Nowhere else in this wide world can you make your
dreams come true
Like you can here in America with hard work, faith and
fortitude

So when you are out there protesting and wanting our
ways to change
Take time to look around the world and see what you
might get in exchange

So, today I will leave my home with my small problems
all packed away
Because without a doubt I'm blessed to live in the world's
greatest country, "AMERICA" today

Helping Hand

I was sitting in the doctor's office patiently waiting for my
turn
I had not a clue about the tragic news I was about to learn

I will never forget the image of the look he gave to me
It was a look of total desperation of what he had just seen

The news to me was devastating and I was in a terrible
mess
The prognosis it was cancer, worse than I could ever guess

I walked from the office knowing my future, it was very
bleak
My life was now in turmoil and but a cure I had to seek

I will never forget how life changed on that dreadful day
Things that were important before to me just seemed to
fade away

I knew I had to fight this battle with all the strength and
faith I had
I refused to not win this fight and leave my daughter
without her dad

Some people choose to face this disease without the will to
fight
But to me I chose to give everything I had and fight with
all my might

continued

Now as I look back on this time and the long and painful
war
I am thankful for the experience, as it changed me for
evermore

My life now is full of happiness, and I am a much better
loving man
So maybe it was just God's way of giving me, that needed
helping hand

Last Thing You See

As I look across the country meadow covered with
morning dew
And I see the sun rising and bringing with it another day
anew

I don't give much thought to how special it is to see this
beautiful site
Or to look at the midnight sky and stars that shine ever so
bright

All of the little things that we all see throughout our busy
day
What would our life be like if all of sudden they went
away

What if you woke this morning and no longer could see
the sun
Would you want the last thing you saw to be beautiful or
fun

Some of us may want to see a peaceful mountain stream
Or the waves splashing on the beach as our final scene

Maybe it would be the clouds forming in the clear blue sky
It might even be seeing your mother cooking her apple pie

We all have different things that we would want as our last
to see
But to me it would be as simple as my family sitting there
with me

Marble Bench

The day was kind of misty and overcast I would say
I was traveling through Miami trying to find my way

There was no GPS back then, so I had to read a map
I was getting tired and weary and I needed a little nap

In the middle of the city hidden under the swaying palm
trees
Was one of the most peaceful beautiful places I have ever
seen

As if I was drawn there by someone that knew I was in
need
It was a very strange feeling, not bad but very loving, yes
indeed

This was an old Monastery showing beauty and grace from
age
The garden gate was open and welcoming with Mary there
on her stage

As I walked down the path alone through the gardens of
this holy place
I came upon this marble bench saying please sit awhile I
have space

It was a very special time of my life fore I knew my life
would be fine
As I sat alone and spoke about my life I could feel God's
hand in mine

continued

In that peaceful garden my problems all seemed to just
fade away
On that marble bench with God in the Monastery on that
drizzly day

Mountain Fire and Memories

Just sitting by the outside fire breathing the mountain air
Thinking about things from my past wishing I was there

Things I did growing up like jumping rope and riding
bikes
And how life was so simple back when we were little
tykes

Then as we grow older with age things begin to change
You have worry about paying bills and other things we
must arrange

We get so busy with our lives just getting through each
and every day
Before you know it without a blink life's good times have
passed away

We hustle off to work every day because we have to pay
the bills
Sometimes forgetting the importance of our children's
daily thrills

The best thing my daughter ever said to me when she was
grown and moved away
Is thank you for the time You and Mom always spent
being there to see her play

continued

So take the time to laugh and talk with your family and
your friends
Fore these are the times you will cherish most when your
life it does end

If Life Had a Re-write

Have you ever given thought about how your life would be
If you could do it all over again, completely from A to Z

If I could do mine again I might study a lot harder in
school
And maybe not worry so much if I looked really cool

I could have driven a little slower while driving down the
road
Could have saved me lots of money, I could have put away
a load

I could do some things different like not party and drink so
much
Instead of all the hotdogs I could have eaten salads for my
lunch

 Could have worked harder and more hours and made me
more money
But just thinking, to do that I would've been away and
surely missed my honey

Maybe I would have traveled more to do more for my
career
But if my daughter called out daddy I would not have been
there to hear

So in the end I have to say even though everything was not
always right
I would not change a thing in my life if I had the chance
for a life's Re-write

Son for Evermore

The smoke has cleared and wedding bells they no longer
ring
The happy couple have left this town to go do their own
thing

The house it now rests all quite and somewhat a little
lonely
Because in this home now it's just my wife, memories and
I only

Our daughter has grown up now and left home with her
true love
The young man in our eyes is truly a blessing from our
God above

They now will start their own life and family as it all
works out
And hopefully one day we will have grandchildren
running all about

They will come home for the holidays and for this I can
hardly wait
Momma will be running around crazy getting the house all
neat and straight

There will be nothing more exciting than to see them
coming to the door
Because we not only have a daughter now, but a son too
for evermore

Waves on the Pier

Sometimes we all have days that go extremely well
Then we have those others that don't seem to go so swell

It seems throughout our life there are many times that are
so fun
Like days we want to just lie around or maybe play out in
the sun

Then there are the others that no matter how hard you
seem to try
You just want to throw in the towel and curl up, lay down
and cry

We have all had these days, both the good ones and the
bad
And we have all had things happen that were so extremely
sad

But the one thing we all need to do to keep our life in
check
Is take a moment now and then to just sit down and reflect

Reflect on all of the gifts in life that have been given to us
all
Things like the seasons of the year winter, spring, summer
and fall

So as you move through this world at life's ever speeding
pace
Take time to stop and reflect on life at your own very
special place

continued

We all need a place we can just sit and think without
distractions in our ear
Mine's sitting there on the beach watching waves flow
through the pier

Times with Friends and Family

I have times when wonderful memories travel through my
mind
The time playing with my girlfriend in the rain and others
of this kind

I remember Grandpa's birthday picnics with family at the
springs
Cousins from all over would bring chicken along with
other things

We would all run to the ice-cold water and take that fearful
jump
Then swing from the rope that hung above by that old
bank side stump

It is sad things as a child that were fun fade away as we
grow old
We must be mature and responsible this is what we are all
told

The truth is we cannot run as fast and play like we once
did
We can't jump as high or throw a ball as hard as when we
were a kid

As I am growing older these memories seem to pop up
more
It seems the memories of my life are the things that I adore

continued

Not once does the memory of the new car or boat take first
place
But it's memories of friends and family that take up my
mind's space

So when you think about what is important in your life the
older that you grow
Remember times with friends and family are most
important, this is what I know

Hurricane in Florida

The morning news anchors are alive and intense
A hurricane's a coming so prepare your defense

The gas stations are closed with gas not to be found
There is no plywood or bottled water anywhere around

The store shelves are empty of soup, beans and spam
People are buying everything that comes in a can

What would a Florida man do without a storm in his life?
Preparing for another hurricane with his children and wife

He gets all his papers and puts them in a Zip lock bag
Fires up the generator in case the power hits a snag

He puts away the patio furniture, so it won't blow away
Then he sits back and waits on the storm coming his way

Then he drinks all his beer and eats all the good snacks
Till nothing is left but spam and beans in the survival sack

So, as he sits in desperation wondering where to buy beer
Thinking this cat 4 hurricane really is nothing to fear

He jumps in the truck fighting off the wind and the rain
When you're out of beer and pork rinds it overrides the
brain

After his journey dodging some fallen trees and down
power lines
Florida man makes it home and through another hurricane
just fine

Parents Not Guns

Another day with more shootings happening out in the
street
An innocent bystander or cop shot while patrolling his beat

This seems to be the times that we all now have to endure
And it seems that politicians chase votes instead of a true
cure

They say take the guns away, yes that will be the mend
But this will not even begin to bring this killing to an end

As we look at all of the root problems of our society today
Taking rights from law abiding Americans will never be
the way

The cure will only begin under the roof of each and every
home
When parents take responsibility for properly raising their
very own

Children today are not taught respect for what others might
believe
They want instant gratification and hate anyone that does
not agree

The respect for teachers and police have all but
disappeared
And the sad part is that it seems to get worse every year

continued

So, before the self-righteous politicians jump at a stupid
newsworthy fix
They need to face the hard truth instead of what is good
for politics

As my mother once told me in her well-meaning way
It's up to parents to teach their children respect and to live
in a proper way

When Those Towers Fell

 7:00 AM that morning when they said goodbye and left
for work
Some were police and fireman while others were innocent
office clerks

The sky was such beautiful blue that morning not a cloud
to be found
As they all walked the city streets cabs and horns were the
only sound

Others rushed through airport lines so they would not miss
their flight
One thing they had in common was they all just woke
from their last night

Little did all of these heroes know this would be their final
day
History was about to change and their lives were the price
to pay

In just an instant that morning fire filled the New York and
DC sky
With terror and destruction everywhere all you could do is
ask why

How do people get so evil and filled with all of this
terrible hate
That they can just get up and go kill thousands and not
even hesitate

continued

In the end the evil did not win fore Americans all came to
their aid
Heroes filled the streets and recruiting offices as if in a big
parade

Our enemies around the world keep trying to cast their
hateful speech
Against the greatest nation on earth where opportunity is
what we teach

A message to all the radical forces who teach and push this
hatred spell
America will never forget the lost lives and the heroes of
when those towers fell

An Electric Car

Flicking through the news today Something caught my eye
It was the political talking heads telling us what to drive

They tell us if we don't join the band evil people we must
be
What's it about driving an electric car that just doesn't
interest me

I don't want to drive a car that doesn't make a sound
I want to it to let me know when I press the throttle down

I want to drive until my gas gauge is damn near on the E
Then I can panic as I look for gas with my wife reminding
me

I don't want to sit at Circle K while my car it gets a charge
If I did, I would eat to many roller dogs and my waist
would get too large

So, I guess I don't want the inconvenience of facing
lifestyle change
And constantly looking for a battery charger that sits
within my cars range

And what if I run out of electricity and my car it seizes to
run
How long would I have to wait for help in the blazing
Florida sun

No, I'll just get into my gas guzzler truck and burn up lots
of gas
And if that doesn't suit you politicians, well you can kiss
my ass

Weeds in the Garden

I just walked out in the yard to plan my yard work for the
day
And noticed weeds had cropped up where I can't let them
stay

When you think about how the world works it all makes
perfect sense
Like weeds growing in the flower garden and covering
beauty so dense

You see negativity are the weeds that grow everyday there
in our mind
They will get out control and continue to take over if we
just stand behind

The negative thoughts and emotions we all have each and
everyday
Will remain on the forefront of your life if they're not
forced to go away

We all have the same issues in our life whether finance,
health or love
But we can choose to let them control our life or fly away
like a dove

continued

The decision isn't really hard to make and it's solely up
you
How you live your life today negative or positive is yours
to choose

So like the weeds that take over the roses and strangle that
beautiful site
You too can let negativity take over and strangle your
wonderful life

Respect, is it Still Here

I was at a gathering yesterday where lots of folks were
there
It was sad to see ladies with their food seeking to find a
chair

The room was full of men sitting that had grown to mature
adult age
Yet none had learned the basics of what my Mom taught
us each day

That was just a simple rule of manners we all should have
been taught
Like learning to eat with a fork and spoon and giving a
lady your spot

This is nothing unusual in the world today which I find it
sad to say
Respect and manners of our tradition all seem to have
passed away

My mother didn't have a lot of riches, not in a monetary
way
But in our home good manners were expected that's all
I've got to say

She taught that people's impression of you are based how
you act
Not on how much money or not that you have there in
your sack

So, take a time when you are out to try to complete only a
minor feat
Like holding a door, removing your hat or giving a lady
your seat

Pauper or a King

"I wonder what the future will bring" is something we
have all asked
It may have been yesterday last year or at another time in
our past

There is only one thing in our life that can provide the
answer to this
That is you and you alone, with personal drive and true
desire to persist

We all control our own future, both the good times and the
bad
We also create how we approach our life either happy or
maybe sad

Life is full of challenges for us that we will face each and
every day
The choice of what your future will bring depends on how
you choose to play

You can choose to lie down and whimper and let your
sorrows beat you down
Or get up wipe off the dust, put on a smile and get rid of
that awful frown

My mother she once told me that we create our own path
in life
And no one else can control yours if you stand up and
fight

continued

So, the next time that you sit and ponder just what your future will bring
Remember only you can in your mind decide whether to be a pauper or a king

What If

What would you do if our world suddenly changed today
A bomb, natural disaster or something else unexplained

Do you have a plan at hand that you can turn to right now
Have the means and food to feed and protect your family
somehow

Do you know how you would live with no electric no cars
or gas
Can you hunt and fish for survival as they did in
generations past

This may sound farfetched and crazy but it may be closer
than we think
With nuclear weapons in the hands of lunatics it could
happen very quick

The big cities will turn to war zones as the lawless will
come to rise
Some of us know how to hunt and fish therefore may
survive

So take a different strategic look at the lifestyle you now
live
For one day your life just may depend on it in the event of
"WHAT IF"

This Old House Was Spared

As I drove through my old neighborhood just the other day
I slowed to a stop in the road and couldn't seem to look
away

What I was looking at was more than just shingles paint
and wood
It was memories of my family and these memories there
are good

This was the house where I lived throughout my youthful
years
It was a place of peace and comfort and where I even shed
a few tears

We would run and play with friends that lived up and
down our red clay street
And at night climb into bed with our windows open while
we went to sleep

Supper time we all ate at the kitchen table and talked about
our day
Momma took turns to listen to what each of us kids had to
say

We all did our part with dishes and cleaning up from
supper time
Not helping with the dishes in our house to Momma was a
crime

continued

We all had our chores to do and school was a major
responsibility
Our Momma insisted that everything be done to your best
ability

I sat there remembering the good times this old house has
shared
I'm thankful that though years and growth this old house
was spared

The Love Drifts Away

There you were standing across that dimly lit crowded
room
You couldn't resist the draw as their eyes gazed at you

That moment changed your lives beyond your wildest
dream
Nothing could ever stop this feeling though to you it
seemed

Your lives went from separate lives and then they become
one
Times were spent sharing love with days and nights of fun

You had the joy of bringing into the world a precious new
life
Years of happiness were shared between children, husband
and wife

Then somehow something changed slowly through all the
years
The days and nights of love slowly turned to times of sad
tears

In life it seems that this happens in love all too many times
What was once the light of your life no longer seeming to
shine

So, you can accept what is happening and let your love go
astray
Or you can fight each day to save your love before it drifts
away

The Florida Pines

Some people love the noise, hustle and bustle of a big city
life
They love riding the subway and all of the buildings and
the lights

Then there are others that crave for the Mountains covered
with white snow
They love to bundle up in winter boots and scarfs when
they have somewhere to go

We also have those people that like to live and play in the
dry desert air
I don't understand it, since nothing but sand and Cactus
growing everywhere

Don't get me wrong, I love the excitement of a New York
City theater at night
The yellow cabs with horns all blowing and Time Square,
Wow what a great site

But when I want to settle down at home there is only one
place for me
That is out in the country of old Florida in the woods by a
lake or stream

Yes, I have to say there is nothing more peaceful than
watching a full moon shine
While swinging with a cold beer and fire at your feet
among the swaying Florida Pines

Surely Fade Away

When we all come into this world, we need help with our
every need
The things in life are learned by all, but at different times
and speed

As we grow through our youth it seems like our life will
never end
But some will die young and we all find this hard to
comprehend

Some lives will be lost from disease while others will
sadly go from drugs
There will be friends and family that leave us on holidays
for heaven above

Some of us will leave this world from needless violence or
an act of war
While others will just fade away in their night's sleep and
wake nevermore

There are those of us that will have to bear the pain while
our children die
For others they will watch their Mom and Dad slowly fade
away and gently cry

The thought of death is something from which we all seem
to want to hide
But the reality is that we will all face death one day, and
this cannot be denied

continued

So, as you go through life share your love with your family each and everyday
Because it is certain that one day, maybe even today, the lives of us all will surely fade away

Mother's Day Upon Us

Here we are again, another year has now quickly come and
gone
Time seems to fly when each day for you starts at first sign
of dawn

You start by fixing breakfast, giving baths and getting
everyone out the door
While picking up the aftermath of toys and clothes left
there on the floor

You get your precious cargo buckled up safely in the car to
leave
Then you run back in the house to get the rest of what you
need

You aren't worried about the problems of the world or
what's on the TV news
To you the most important thing are do the kids have on
socks and matching shoes

Oh yes you are running at warp speed every day from
daylight until after dark
Whether off to school functions, doctor appointments,
fixing supper or birthday at the park

Most people think motherhood is an easy life and always
full of joy and fun
But it takes a huge commitment to carry, give birth and to
raise that precious little one

Some mothers work a job in addition while some have to
raise their children all alone

continued

These mothers should not be looked down upon but placed
high upon a throne

Oh yes motherhood isn't easy and I can't think of a more
selfless rewarding task
If you don't believe me, just find any mother out there,
stop them and just ask

What A Grandfather Should Be

I was sitting alone at a restaurant table eating lunch today
When there came an elderly man walking slowly as if to
find his way

He reminded me of my grandfather who years ago had
passed
Not by his moving slowly but it was his white shirt and his
hat

Growing up in our home next door to him was such a great
way live
There was never anything we kids could want he wasn't
willing to give

No, I'm not talking about the material things that it took
money to buy
I'm talking of all the time he gave to have us grandkids all
there by his side

He would get up each and every morning and get dressed
to the tee
He would put on a white starched shirt and fedora hat this
I guarantee

He may have been working in the yard or going to Rich's
Country Store
Where saw dust was on the butcher's floor and cookie jars
were there to adore

continued

No matter if his day was keeping him close home or taking
him somewhere afar
He would never leave home by himself as he would pile us
grandkids all in the car

Yes, my grandfather was a man I truly loved and was a
great role model to me
From him I learned the true value of family and what a
grandfather should be

Best Meal I Ever Ate

I have been very fortunate traveling throughout my life's
many days
I have traveled and had the opportunity to dine in oh so
many ways

I have enjoyed a taco in Texas and BBQ from one of
Memphis best
A steak at Rockefeller Center and amazing smothered
chicken breast

In the woods I've even eaten squirrel roasted fresh over an
open fire
And I can't forget the apple turnovers Grandma just took
from the frier

But up on the top of the list of fine dining that I've
experienced in my life
Is a little restaurant on the Georgia roadside that I can
never seem to pass by

Oh, this little buffet in Georgia has the best fried fish or
fried chicken halve
But you have to get there early or a table and chair you
will not have

With butter beans, fried okra and biscuits piled high in
chicken and fish
This is a feast that rates at the top of every country boy's
greatest wish

continued

But best of all is the bonus, that's always stacked there by
the front door
Boxes of fresh Georgia grown tomatoes like you have
never tasted before

So when you ask me, "Bobby what's the best meal that
you have ever ate"
It's the Georgia Tomato with Mayo on white bread right
here on my plate

Live For Today

Well yesterday was filled with memories, some fun and
some were sad
I saw old school mates from my youth and to catch up, for
this I was glad

Funny how lives they venture down different roads,
throughout our separate lives
Some have taken their life slowly, while others live theirs
as living in overdrive

It's been a long time since we all ventured out to chase our
separate dreams
Some to serve our country, some to corporate and some in
business it seems

But the one thing that is constant is there is tragedy,
existing in everyone's life
Maybe financial, health, lost a sibling, a child or maybe a
husband or a wife

In this world there are no promises or guarantees of what
in our life we'll see
So we have to accept our challenges along the way and
remain happy as can be

I for one can honestly say there were choices made that
maybe were not the best
But looking back I wouldn't change a single one for it may
have affected the rest

continued

So, as we grow into our golden years remember the joys
you have had along the way
And forget the tragedies that occurred along the road and
get out and live for today

If We Knew it was Our Last

As I drive here all alone with tears running from my eyes
Dealing with the news and this awful unforeseen surprise

Thinking back about our conversation on the couch just
the other day
When you were speaking, and my eyes they just drifted far
away

What you were saying was very important at that time in
your mind
But to me it really didn't seem to matter much, it was just
a waste of time

How many times have we been through this situation in
our married life
Where we took for granted the times that are spent just
husband and a wife

Then one day you get the news that your loved ones not
coming home
Maybe you had a chance to say good-by or maybe they left
this world alone

None of us know if our time on earth will end tomorrow or
today
But chances are when it comes you will always have more
to say

You will wish you had been more attentive to what they
said just the other day
You will cry and wish you could have talked some more
before they went away

continued

Yes, if in this life we only knew that this time for us, it
would be the last
If we only knew that tomorrow our world would fall apart
and change just that fast

We would embrace every moment that we have to share
with the ones we love
So, treat every day as the last, for one day, Your love will
be called home from above

Calluses and Dirty Hands

From the day you are born your parents preach every day
They tell you being a Doctor or Lawyer, yes that's the best way

They say go to college and get your degree
Your life will be good then, this you will see

But when we look around there are so many paths
Thank goodness college wasn't in everyone's past

When you look around this country at everything you see
You see schools, bridges and houses built for you and me

As you sit at the table and enjoy tonight's meal
Just give a short thanks to the farmer in the field

When you leave home in your car to drive your child to school
Remember your car wasn't built by a lawyer, but by a man with tools

Some people look down at workers with hands covered with grease
But you need to remember without them progress would cease

Yes, this ole world get by just fine without the men wearing suits
But would stop in a second without the men that wear gloves and boots

continued

These hard workers build, farm and are the backbone of
our land
So, I thank God for the man with calluses and dirt on their
hands

Growing Up in a Small Town

Life was much simpler and times they were fun
Summer days in the lake to beat the heat and the sun

We wore cut off blue jeans and shoes were never worn
We just used our pocketknife if we stepped on a thorn

Saturdays the kids all rode downtown on our bikes
Get ice cream at the drug store and watch a movie we
liked

After supper kids washed dishes and watched TV together
With 3 channels and no remote we just watched whatever

Curfew by our parents when on a date Saturday Night
Were all firmly set and upheld for the stroke of midnight

No stores open Wednesday afternoon or Sunday at the
time
And nowhere on Sunday could you ever buy beer or wine

Friday night football games were the event of the week
To all of us kids the players were true heroes I think

Neighbors looked after the kids as if they were their own
And if you caused a problem the word would beat you
home

The parents they knew all of the kids that would come
around
Yep, life sure was great growing up in my small town

How Time Flies

This morning I'm sitting here enjoying my coffee all by
myself
And happened to glance at the pictures there on the
bookshelf

The pictures on the shelf varied of different times from our
past
But the one thing that hit me was how the time goes by so
fast

Yes, there is a picture of us at a party from many years ago
Then there is the one of my brother and sisters that I love
so

The thing that I see isn't the pictures and frames on display
No, it's how fast the time has flown by while life's on it's
way

It seems as if only yesterday that these poses in the
pictures took place
But, in reality it was years ago that seem to have flown fast
through space

Time has a way of slipping from us with the daily grind of
our life
And it seems to fly by faster with each year, I only wish I
knew why

Groves Have Gone Away

Leaving town this morning something jumped out in my
mind
About how things have changed and old times, just got left
behind

When I was just a young boy growing up in the Florida
sand
There were not all these houses and condos scattered all
over this land

There were vast beautiful orange groves from the east
coast to the west
Tangerines and Florida navels growing everywhere, oh
they were the best

We grew up running through the groves and eating
oranges sitting in the trees
Even used to go parking with our girlfriends in the grove
in the midnight breeze

Then one day it happened and the mouse landed here in
town
Then before we knew it the orange groves they were all
mowed down

Houses, motels and condos were now popping up
everywhere
And amusement parks now take the place of groves that
once were there

continued

It's sad to see how our state has changed and our heritage
it's now gone
Florida is now just a tourist state and farmers they have all
moved on

I know in my heart that progress is something that we can
never stop
But it would be nice to see an orange grove instead of a T-
Shirt shop

Front Porch

I always love to drive slow though these little southern
towns
And I always turn off the main street and just wonder
around

There are lots of homes with front porches with two
rocking chairs there
They all look so warm and inviting, like saying come sit
and visit me here

You don't see many houses built with front porches these
days
The days of sitting on the front porch seem to have all
gone away

My Mom was always on her porch, seemed like from
morning till night
When you would ride by and see her there you knew she
was alright

At some point front porches gave way to backyards
surrounded by fence
People became more private and around neighbors and
uptight and tense

Times they have changed now, the neighbors we don't
know or even care
Yes, I think we would all be better off with a front porch
with two rocking chairs

Moments

I just heard something said that really hit home with me
It made me stop and think of what life's all about you see

Our life shouldn't be about a big home, a boat or new car
It should be about memories both common and the bazaar

Life is about the times we spend with our family and
friends
Memories made of special times, we remember till the end

The first Christmas with your newborn or last with your
Mom
Flying a kite in the rain with your new love on the college
lawn

Yes, these are the things that make life fun and fulfilled
The memories of times past that always gave us a thrill

So, as you move through your days and your life it moves
on
Remember to cherish those special moments as you move
along

Weathered and Frail

Today I was in search of a certain old picture, all to no
avail
But came upon a very special picture of something
weathered and frail

It wasn't an old baseball mitt or old worn-out football
shoes
And not anything of value that anyone of us would ever
use

It was something that looked rough and had seen it's share
of hard times
To just look at them you would never know that they had
such a hard climb

No, these rough little things had fought a hard life that
most could never bear
They had experienced some dire hardships but to family,
they always were there

There were times they were there open with love for us
kids to hold on
And others to point the right direction when we did
something wrong

Through life these two weathered little hands had carried
such a big demanding load
And I'll always cherish that picture of my mother's little
hands the day she let life go

What Shall I Do

I was folding clothes from the dryer just now

When something hit me that is a major problem for me
somehow

Just then I suddenly noticed something was just not the
same

All of my underwear and socks were old with holes and
that's such a shame

No new socks and underwear for Christmas, I just don't
understand

I didn't even get a single damn pair out of Santa Clause's
hand

Now I have two choices to deal with in my simple life

Go buy some myself or maybe I can ask a favor of my
wife

I don't know where you actually buy these things since
there was never a need to know

Since for Christmas each and every year I knew I was
always good to go

Well, guess I'll put on a pair of socks a hole in the toe and
drawers with a hole in the ass

And go to Walmart or Target and stock up for myself and
better do it real fast

Exercise He Said

So, the other day the Doctor told me I need to exercise
some more
But I really find exercising every day to be such a terrible
bore

So I asked the good Doctor what did he personally
recommend
And he said for me to ride a bike, walk or maybe start to
swim

I started my search for something that was of interest to
me
It couldn't be real hard or hot and make me sweat don't
you see

If I decided to swim at the Y people probably have peed in
the pool
And if I put on speedo people would laugh and I'd look
like a pervert or fool

No, swimming I don't see working for me or very good fit
But walking may be OK, hell I can stop and take a rest
every little bit

Then I started thinking about maybe buying me one of
these fancy new bikes
That seems like something fun and not too hard to do that I
might really like

continued

So I bought me a bike and one of those outfits with a
helmet and tight-fitting shorts
And took off looking good in my shorts for a long ride
around the town lake shore

You know this exercise stuff, if my crotch doesn't chafe it
ain't all that damn bad
But if the battery on this electric bike dies and I have to
pedal I will be extremely mad

I Don't Know the Pronouns

I was with a group of people just the other day
When I was told by someone there be careful what you say

You see some people today are offended if you use the
wrong word or term
They will get real mad and cry if you disagree with what
they learned

They say you must use certain pronouns to fit in with
society today
That can be a problem since I don't know what pronoun I
can say

You see I wasn't that good in school and English that's for
sure
So I'm not sure what a pronoun does and a lesson I can't
endure

I really don't understand why people today always get so
upset
They act like little children when offended and break out
in a sweat

So, all I have to say to this is If I use the wrong pronoun
and you I offend
Grow up and get a life, because I really don't care and
won't until the end

Song In Our Mind

I woke up this morning with a song from my past playing
in vividly my head
I got in my truck and turned up the song as I drove down
the road ahead

This song it brought back memories of a special time in
my younger years
Ever since that time years ago, this song, it's been
embedded in my ears

What makes a song stay with us and return unexplained
time to time
And bring with it the vivid image of that special time and
place in our mind

We all have these songs that bring back visions every time
that special one we hear
Might be of that first date or that night making love on the
beach with someone dear

The memories that are projected by that special song can
never be explained
When you combine a song and special time its etched
forever there in your brain

So just turn up the music and enjoy this magical ride
traveling back into your past
I just remember about how at that time, you wished that
special time would forever last

Eyes From the Heart

I recently saw a drawing and the effect on me at the time, I
was unaware
But the vision of what it said to me has since followed me
everywhere

This piece of beautiful art wasn't a Picasso masterpiece
Or from Salvador Dali or the Mona Lisa, not at all, don't
you see

This simple little drawing told a most valuable lesson of
how to live our life
It was so plain without even a word written or spoken to
me that night

It resonated like nothing else and would change the way
we live life, it seems to me
This masterpiece of art had our eyes connected to our
heart, instead of our brain you see

Rain Like the Memories

Staring from my porch watching the rain through the early
morning light
As it came down through the trees and the meadow was
such a peaceful site

I couldn't help but notice how the trees and grass suddenly
were bright green
With the dust of the dry hot days washed away and leaves
left with a bright sheen

The rain to trees and plants are the nourishment they need
to flourish and survive
Much like the love of a companion that provides drive and
purpose to us in our life

We all need that someone that like the rain gives us
strength to grow and endure
Through the dry times in our lives when our mind fills
with dust and we feel insecure

Some of us are fortunate enough to have that someone
always there at hand
While others have seen theirs drift away like the desert's
blowing sand

Whether yours is standing there with you today or just a
precious memory of the past
The effect like the rain has on the trees and grass the
support and memories will forever last

Money on the Way

I went to the mailbox looking for some good news I
thought would arrive today
I am waiting on my PCH million dollar winnings I might
have won I heard the man on TV say

Now I don't think the TV spokesman would be dishonest
and lie to me
Because I ordered the magazine subscription that they
presented to improve my chances, don't you see

The email said I was a finalist and needed to watch closely
for the mail
I called the bank and told them to get ready for a surprise
of which I cannot tell

I think I might go ahead and buy me a new boat or maybe
even a new sports car
Because I feel for sure my check's in the mail and by next
week I'll be living like a big time movie star

Hard to Endure

Some go through life taking most things in stride
While others choose to live with humor and joy all
wrapped up inside

I never understood why people choose to always be
unhappy and sad
When it is just as easy to spend your time being thankful
and glad

I look at each day as a blessing to cherish and hold
To look at life with laughter instead of bitter and cold

Not everything we touch in life goes according to plan
But we play the cards we are dealt and hope for a better
hand

I've never seen a situation where a bad attitude helped you
to win
But possibilities are endless with a light hearted outlook
and grin

So I will close my eyes tonight and be thankful for the joy
in my life
While others will lay awake fighting drama and sorrow
under the bedside light

When the morning sun arises again the choice will be
yours
Wake up cheerful and happy or face a day hard to endure

Ice Cream Truck

This always seems to happen to us all when we grow up
from our youth
Our mind begins to get cluttered with life and that's the
unfortunate truth

When we were young and we were carefree, we had
experiences beyond belief
Our problems that came to us each day were minor and
most were very brief

The biggest issue that we faced were a skinned knee or
maybe flat tire on our bike
Or maybe having to build up nerve to call the girl in our
class that we really liked

But as we grow older and into adults and we struggle
through our daily grind
We need to just slow down a little and remember our
youth, and times we left behind

As I witnessed the smile of joy today on my
granddaughter's face as it beamed
There couldn't be a better time for them than there with
Dad, eating ice cream truck ice cream

So, take a little time each day to reminisce about your
youth and maybe with a little luck
You again, may enjoy the sounds and flavors of your
childhood at an ice cream truck

Old Box of Memories

The other day I was killing time watching the tree
limbs in the breeze gently sway
When I noticed an old box of photographs that
long ago had been stored away

I don't know what drove me to dig the box out and
spread it out on the bedroom floor
But I'm sure glad I did because that box held a
lifetime of smiles for me, that's for sure

There were photos of family members I didn't
remember or maybe even know
Pictures of toddlers and Moms in Easter dresses
with their Easter baskets there in tow

I saw pictures of my father and his army buddies
dirty and tired during the war
They were smiling and appeared to be waiting for
what next for them, was in store

Pictures of our dining table my young bride
prepared for our first meal as a new team
That folding table and chairs with candles was
more beautiful than I could ever dream

And then there were the memories with our
daughter as she continued to grow
Her smiles and how proud we always were
through those photos will always show

Continued

Yes, I got back some precious memories of special times
of love and laughter of my youth
And I can't be thankful enough for the wonderful life I've
had and that's the solemn truth

Roadside Cross

While driving down this lonely backwoods road today
I came upon a pitiful site there in the left side right of way

A lady was sitting on an old homemade pink wooden bench
Just staring at the faded flowers and cross next to the trench

The bench it was flacking, and paint it was severely worn
The flowers were all faded and ribbon, it was all frayed and torn

I couldn't help but think to myself how long it had been in place
Or how many times in her life she had come to visit this same space

Was it a child that was lost in a tragic accident or someone else that she loved
Did she come here everyday of her life to ask why of the Lord above

Maybe it was just her quite place that gave her hope and solemn peace
Just sitting under the oak tree staring at faded flowers of blue and green

We all have our special way of dealing with tragedy that we don't understand
Hers was talking to the faded flowers and roadside cross that behind them stands

Vincent's Five and Dime

Some of us still live in the small town, the one where we
were raised
While others have moved on to places, where others would
be amazed

Some of us grew up on the city streets of a big city full of
people on the go
While others played on a Main Street with nothing special
to really show

I grew up in that little town where everyone knew your
name
Where every Saturday the kids all gathered and did just the
same

We rode our bikes downtown to the soda fountain, that's
no longer there
And paid a nickel at the State Theater for popcorn, that we
had to share

I will always remember the site of new bikes at the
Western Auto on display
And the feeling of getting a new gun and holster with caps
ready to play

One day my wife and I chose to move back to that little
town that we call home
To raise our daughter in a place where we felt she was safe
to get out and roam

Though things have changed in this small town as they
always do over time
I still see these stores in my mind Harper's, Ferran's,
Acie's and Vincent's Five and Dime

Down on Your Knees

Watching the news again last night, the same as I often do
Listening to what our politicians are doing to help me and
you

I learned that inflation is coming down and we are all in
good shape
And all we have to do is vote for them again and just sit
back and wait

We will see how good things will be if we just listen, and
with them agree
With new policy it no longer get hot in July or cold in
December this you will see

We no longer need our gas guzzling cars to go on that
vacation trip
Or that terrible gas stove to cook breakfast eggs or supper
shrimp

No, we just need to remember to do as we are told and not
cause a fuss
Because we all know our politicians are smarter and will
do what's best for us

I'm not sure where it's all going and I guess we'll just
have to wait and see
But just for safety sake you might want bow your head and
get down on your knees

Get Them Out of the Way

There used to be a time in history when adults could work
their differences out
They could talk, maybe duel, then shake hands and walk
away without a scream or shout

Then someone decided we needed politicians, to tell us all
what we should do
Because everyone knows these officials know better what's
best for me and you

Then they got their buddies to go get law degrees, this
would help us all you see
And for a fee they would use big words and determine
who's right , is it you or is it me

So then we had our politicians who got an office and
managed to stay there for life
And lawyers to create legal decisions with big words that
only they can understand or write

Yes, our life went to hell in a hurry with these two
anointed groups
Politicians bickering with each other with lawyers waiting
for someone to sue

Yes, if we want to make our life a lot more simple and live
a happier life today
A good start would be setting term limits for politicians
and getting lawyers out of the way

Labor Day

Labor Day is more important than most will ever see
People don't care why, it's just a day off work it seems

Well it's a day to celebrate the laborers that are the
backbone of this land
The ones that get their hands dirty and all day on their feet
they stand

These are the people that built this great land with hard
work and sweat of their brow
And managed to get out production when needed working
long hard hours somehow

They will always be the strength and heart of this great
land that we all enjoy
Building cars and houses or maybe even your child's
favorite Christmas toy

Yes the one with strong arms and dirty callused hands is
the true hero I admire
And to think they are sometimes be looked down upon by
the ones educated higher

So we all to need to remember that without labor, this
country would not exist
So I promise to stand and defend their honor, with heart
and soul and fist

OPRY HOUSE

Opry House and Soda Shop

We've all seen these places, that just seem to have been
lost in time
The new four lane highway came along, and it just passed
it by

As I sit here alone and gaze down this lonely empty
overgrown lane
In my mind I can envision years ago, when it wasn't near
the same

I see that time so many years ago, that have flown by us
now
When the empty buildings were bustling with people in
this little town

The old Opry House had a packed house at the show on
Saturday night
While the little corner drug store was busy dipping ice
cream they liked

Yes, it is sad these lost little towns are idle and just left to
fade away
While their wooden sidewalks and painted store windows
have yet to decay

It's as if the wood sidewalks and painted store windows
refuse to let go and die
Almost as if they are begging for help for revival, from
strangers who pass bye

Continued

But as we know, life goes on, and the progress, I know it
will never stop
I just hope my grandkids will one day see, this old Opry
house and corner soda shop

CAFE

Whistle Stop

If you are driving through middle Georgia and at noon
you're ready to eat
You need to swing by this little hole in the wall that's
really pretty neat

It sits at the end of this little forgotten lost in time one
street town
Where you will see the 1892 Opry House and Court House
and never have to move around

I have to tell you if it's Creme Brule or escargot that you
want for your lunch
Then this probably isn't the place you want stop your car,
maybe just a hunch

No this is the place for fried green tomatoes with meat loaf
and hot cornbread
Or maybe just a light lunch of a fried green tomato grilled
cheese with sweet iced tea instead

It became a national landmark with the help of movie fame
While the menu specialty gave this Hollywood classic it's
famous name

So the next time you're hungry and are near little Juliette,
GA
Stop and eat some fried green tomatoes at the Whistle
Stop Cafe

Under the Bridge

Two brothers grew up together playing every day in the
home backyard
Life following in each other's path when young really
wasn't very hard

But as they grew their paths in life they began to change
How two brothers end up in such different places, to me it
seems so strange

One brother went away to medical school and married his
college flame
While the other's life took a tragic path which is such a
terrible shame

One brother chose to proudly fight for our land to protect
and keep us free
While the other spent his days injecting Botox where
pretty people felt the need

Tonight one is sleeping with his bride in a fancy bed up on
society ridge
While the forgotten other who fought to protect us all is
sleeping cold under the I-10 bridge

My Life Path

I am sitting here and analyzing my current place in life
About how my life has evolved and I got my lovely wife

It got me thinking about if our life, is it all pre-planned
Is our life pre-determined like a road map drawn in the
sand

From the first moment that I appeared on this earth as a
newborn babe
Was it already set in stone that I would be sitting here
today

Was it all laid out up front and my decisions, were they all
pre-approved
As if no matter what I think or want, from my path I can't
be removed

Or maybe is it all up to us how we choose to live our life
That we are free to make our own choices anyway that we
like

I don't know and never will know the answer I suppose
For there is only one person I can think of, that for sure
really knows

Ride in my Mind

I took a ride in my mind today to a special place in time
Beachbound on highway 44 with a load of friends of mine

Surfboards on the roof tied down and baggies are what we wore
We left home at break of dawn to see what today the waves had in store

How much fun we had at the beach when there we did finally land
Gathering with our friends on the waves and playing in the soft white sand

From daylight until late at night we partied there on the beach
Way down at the inlet Getty where most others could not reach

We were there in our own little world with not a care in site
Just enjoying our teenage life and love way into the night

The 8-track blaring music from Led Zepplin and Rolling Stones
Lying in the moonlight with your love never wanting to go home

Today I'm driving on 44 again heading to that same beach town
This time with my laptop and no surfboard on the roof tied down

continued

It's funny how fast times they changed from this different
world
From our carefree teenage years to adults in such a hectic
whirl

So I think I'll crank up Led Zepplin and let wind blow
through my hair
And happily think about those carefree times until my
appointment I get there

Coming Home

I came out of a little restaurant after lunch the other day
And decided to take a seat on the sidewalk bench before
driving on my way

An well-dressed gentleman approached and asked if he
could have a seat
He said he might be a while for his wife he was waiting to
meet

She was at that fancy hair salon, you know the one on the
corner down the way
She was getting her hair done because their daughter and
family were coming home today

You see, he said they now live in the city where all the
excitement lies
But have decided they wanted a better life for the kids,
much to our surprise

They wanted their kids to grow up where teachers and
principles knew all the children's names
And the town would turn out to support the children in
their plays and games

He said when his daughter told her mother he had never
seen her so glad
Yes, she said they were moving their kids back to this little
town for a life just like she had

Country Buffet

There isn't anything like it in a small southern town that
brings everyone together
We see elderly lady in pearls with a walker sitting with a
biker dressed in leather

You see a doctor and lawyer sitting and laughing with a
local farmer
And the preacher of the downtown Baptist church with
police in body armor

Everyone seems so content if only for a short while
No cell phones ringing just conversation and a lot of hugs
and smiles

The food is hot and piled up high as you amble past the
delicious feast
Just gazing and trying to decide today what do I want to
eat

That's the atmosphere that is so hard find at most places
today
Yes this is what I love about a small town country style
buffet

Family

Something came to my attention which is very dear to me
It is something not all of us have or some even care about
it seems

It's not the house in which I live or car I get in and drive
You see it's my family that I cherish more than anything in
my life

Though we don't always agree on things, but we always
get along
We will always stick together because our family bond is
so strong

My mother taught me that life can be very tuff and
sometimes it seems unfair
But as I fight life's daily battles I know my family for me
will always be there

We all face struggles and conflicts that are sometimes hard
to overcome
And sometime think we need to leave a family squabble
thinking that we won

But when it's time to leave this world and you are lying
there alone
It may just be too late to get that lost family member on
the phone

So give some thought to what's important in your own life
today
And maybe make up with that family member that you let
slip away

Coconut Soap

I'm not sure when or how this major change took place
But this attack on tradition and manhood is a complete
disgrace

What I'm talking about isn't skinny jeans or men getting a
pedicure
It's much more serious and beyond what a man should ever
have to endure

Yes this has happened in our home as I'm sure it has in
others
It is the start of the fall of manhood for all men and their
brothers

This my friends is the demise of the floating bar of good
old Ivory soap
The soap for men began it's downfall when Old Spice put
it on a rope

Today I got in the shower after working in the yard and
much to my surprise
I came to the realization that life had changed for me and
other guys

There is no longer soap in a bar or even rope soap to be
found
The only soap is coconut that you have to squirt around

What the hell is this all about that now I bath with coconut
and scrunchy sponge
I guess my wife has just won again so I guess I'll just take
the coconut soap plunge

No Longer a Swing

There are some inventions that prove to be great for
society
That over the years seem to achieve great notoriety

These are few and sometimes very far apart
And I'm not speaking of things like electricity or the car

No, I'm speaking of something much more simple and
cheap
Something where young couples created memories to
forever keep

This simple invention was found all over town
On every front porch on the street one could be found

I'm talking of the porch swing where you would sit and
talk about the day
And you could sit and swing and give the neighbors a
friendly wave

Where young couples on their first date would sit and hold
hands
And talk about when they get married and their future
plans

Yes the front porch swing is truly something to behold
Our founders even wrote the constitution on the porch in a
swing is what I've been told

Sadly, a front porch swing's place in time has faded away
and could not last
Because they no longer build a front porch to hang a swing
on homes you drive past

Family Slip By

It was Sunday night in America and everyone was always
home
Laying on the floor in their pajamas the Ed Sullivan Show
for sure was on

It may have been Elvis Presley and they wouldn't dare
show him shake his hips
Or might have been the Beatles with new style rock and
roll coming from their lips

The times they were much simpler all those years ago
The family time together was different then as I'm sure
you all know

Families spent more time together with no social media to
get in the way
With only one phone in the kitchen where everyone could
hear what you had to say

Technology it progresses and I'm first to say for this I'm
glad
But on the other hand what we lose in the transition, this is
very sad

Things will keep getting smarter, smaller and faster it
seems in only a blink of an eye
So while everything is moving so fast try not to let life
with your family slip by

Pride in What You Have

While driving down the back road GA Highway Twenty
Three
I passed a little leaning manicured house sitting back under
the trees

This reminded me of a couple that lived at the end of our
old road
Their little house appeared about to fall down but the yard
was always trimmed and mowed

Their little house was always spotless with nothing out of
place
And you never saw them without a welcoming smile every
day upon their face

These folks didn't have a lot of material things that most of
us all want
No they had no desire for a big old house or a bunch of
stuff around to flaunt

But of what they had they cherished and of it were very
proud
And I can say you could never find better people anywhere
in a crowd

This little man and wife raised a family of four successful
and great sons
Stopping to chat with him under the little leaning shed was
always enlightening and fun

Yes the true definition of success isn't about your wallet
or the money you have in there
But about the love, pride in what you have and the
enjoyment you choose to share

Button Fly Jeans

While traveling south on I-75 just the other day
I had to swing into a rest area there along my way

As I was in the restroom I witnessed something the fear of
every man
A gentleman came in at a fast pace trying to open his pants
with his frantic hand

You see the problem wasn't a physical impairment or that
he could not see
It was his wife had bought him a pair of new skinny fit
button fly blue jeans

He couldn't get the buttons loose and they were to tight for
him to pull down
And he desperately seeked help from anyone else in there
standing around

Well I felt sorry for the guy and understood his
desperate need
But if he needed someone to help unbutton his fly it wasn't
going to be me

Today I still wonder how things turned out for that poor
guy
But I bet at the next Walmart a pair of relaxed fit zipper fly
jeans he definitely did buy

Travel light

Through all the years of traveling the back roads of this
great land
I learned to travel with only a shoulder bag with
underwear, toothbrush and a pair of jeans in my hand

A couple of shirts and a pair jeans will get me through a
week
But when I travel with my bride my back tends to get real
weak

You see she needs to pack clothes for all occasions just in
case the need arise
Ten pairs of shoes, four different coats cause it might get
cold outside

I'm not sure why women pack different than men when on
a trip they go
But it sure makes getting in and out of a hotel room very
hard and slow

The springs on the car cry out in pain when suitcases all go
in
And the car struggles in anguish when the hilly roads
begin

I just don't understand why she needs to take all this stuff
along
She needs to leave these boots and heels and coats and
dresses and jewelry at home where they belong

Smiles

I stopped for supper at this roadside restaurant while on
the road today
The experience at this little diner really made my day

The meal it was very good and portions were immense
But something really made it great and worth all the
dollars and cents

What made the meal so pleasant was nothing on the plate
But the waitress was so polite and her beautiful smile was
special I must say

A smile is something that we all have inside but some
choose not to use
Might think they have a limited number and don't want to
waste one on you

Some people, they are happy and always choose to smile
While others like being down and grim and unhappy all
the while

So remember that it's not hard to smile and maybe make
someone's day
And it just might make you a whole lot happier, there
along the way

Rocks In the River

Sitting here watching the cold water flow over the
beautiful smooth river rocks
This made me think about how life and nature, how
they closely interlock

The water is moving along as usual in a smooth and
calm constant slow flow
Then all of a sudden it hits a bunch of rocks,
everywhere there in the road

The direction suddenly changes and the speed of the
water takes off in a flash
Bouncing over and around the rocks the water comes
down in a turbulent crash

This is like mine and your life that we go through
every day
Things are running along real smooth until pile of
rocks get in the way

But as I look a little way down the river something
becomes very clear to me
The water calms down and flows smooth again just as
in our life it always seems

Forever Cry

As I look at the world and all people that happily live out
there
There are people of different religions and races living
together everywhere

Then there are some people that hate others based on race
or what they believe
Why they want to destroy another for that reason is very
strange to me

You see it really doesn't matter what religion you believe
or what you want to preach
As long as hate for your fellow man is not there in what
you teach

Wars have been fought all through time for no good reason
to me it seems
All have been fought for greed and power or pushing your
beliefs on others like me

So while you choose to hate and kill your neighbors and
happily watch them die
Remember there are innocent people on both sides that
have to hold their dying loved ones and will forever cry

Moon Pie

We all have traditions and foods that are unique to the area
in which we live
Things and foods that are traditional and to all new
generations that we give

When you go New York City you must eat the pizza from
a sidewalk stand
And when in Philadelphia put a Phili cheese steak there in
your hand

When in New Orleans Gumbo and beignet are foods that
you must partake
But while in Chicago a Hot Dog with the works is what
you have for heaven's sake

This brings me to a food staple that has been consumed by
most in the deep south
For over 100 years it has been a must have delicacy that
will melt there in your mouth

Yes I'm talking about a simple treat that is a favorite of all
true southerners from the flat lands to mountains high
It is the favorite snack found in every back road country
store, an RC Cola and Moon Pie

Time

A famous person when he was asked what was the most
valuable asset that he owned
His answer was something that he cherished dearly, but
couldn't be driven or even shown

I walked away from hearing his answer, and it stuck there
in my mind
Just how profound and simple that I couldn't leave the
thought behind

What he said was his most cherished possession is owned
by every one of us today
It is the gift of time that we all have to use or we can just
let it drift away

I realized then how truly rich I am to possess my own
life's bank account of time
Now I will carefully pick and choose how to spend my
riches to get the most from mine

In closing I want to thank everyone that was the inspiration for my writings. You never knew that something you said or did at given point in time would end up in some crazy person's mind, maybe years later and be the inspiration of a writing to be held throughout eternity.

Thank you whoever you are for all the inspiration!

From My World to Yours,
Bob Baker